RRya

HIP-HOP
ARTISTS

FUTURE

RAP RISING STAR

BY MELISSA HIGGINS

Essential Library

An Imprint of Abdo Publishing
abdopublishing.com

ABDOPUBLISHING.COM

Published by Abdo Publishing, a division of ABDO, PO Box 398166, Minneapolis, Minnesota 55439. Copyright © 2018 by Abdo Consulting Group, Inc. International copyrights reserved in all countries. No part of this book may be reproduced in any form without written permission from the publisher. Essential Library™ is a trademark and logo of Abdo Publishing.

Printed in the United States of America, North Mankato, Minnesota
102017
012018

Cover Photo: Rex Features/AP Images
Interior Photos: Shutterstock Images, 4, 25; Matt Sayles/Invision/AP Images, 8, 58–59, 64–65, 71; BG017/Bauer-Griffin/GC Images/Getty Images, 10–11; Prince Williams/FilmMagic/Getty Images, 12, 76–77; Jeff Kravitz/FilmMagic, Inc/Getty Images, 15; Featureflash Photo Agency/Shutterstock Images, 17; Jamie Lamor Thompson/Shutterstock Images, 21, 51, 55, 86; Rex Features/AP Images, 22, 32, 61; David Goldman/AP Images, 28; S. Bukley/Shutterstock Images, 31; Robb D. Cohen/Invision/AP Images, 34–35; Jeff Daly/Invision/AP Images, 39; Donald Traill/Invision/AP Images, 41; Kevin Tachman/Getty Images Entertainment/Getty Images, 42; Prince Williams/WireImage/Getty Images, 46–47, 63, 94–95; Ted S. Warren/AP Images, 48; Scott Kirkland/Invision/AP Images, 52; Owen Sweeney/Invision/AP Images, 66–67; Thaddaeus McAdams/Getty Images Entertainment/Getty Images, 69; Bruce Fleming/AP Images, 74–75; Johnny Nunez/WireImage/Getty Images, 78–79; Ricky Bassman/Cal Sport Media/AP Images, 81; Randy Miramontez/Shutterstock Images, 84; Ovidiu Hrubaru/Shutterstock Images, 89; Charles Sykes/Invision/AP Images, 90–91; Maggie Boyd/Sipa USA/Newscom, 97

Editor: Brenda Haugen
Series Designer: Laura Polzin

PUBLISHER'S CATALOGING-IN-PUBLICATION DATA

Names: Higgins, Melissa, author.
Title: Future: rap rising star / by Melissa Higgins.
Other titles: Rap rising star
Description: Minneapolis, Minnesota : Abdo Publishing, 2018. | Series: Hip-hop artists | Includes online resources and index.
Identifiers: LCCN 2017946870 | ISBN 9781532113284 (lib.bdg.) | ISBN 9781532152160 (ebook)
Subjects: LCSH: Future (Nayvadius DeMun Wilburn), 1983-.--Juvenile literature. | Rap musicians--United States--Biography--Juvenile literature. | Rap (Music)--Juvenile literature.
Classification: DDC 782.421649 [B]--dc23
LC record available at https://lccn.loc.gov/2017946870

CONTENTS

"INCREDIBLE"

Walls slid apart on the stage of the television talk show *Ellen* on March 2, 2017. As a man sporting long dreadlocks and sunglasses was revealed, the studio audience erupted into cheers. The rapper—born Nayvadius Wilburn, but now known as Future—is six feet, three inches (1.9 m) tall, slender, and athletic. He was wearing a sweatshirt displaying the face of rock legend Jimi Hendrix, the inspiration for his most recent album, *HNDRXX*.

In the style of a true MC rapper, Future joyously waved his arm back and forth, getting the crowd worked up. A backup band accompanied him as he bounced across the stage, singing "Hands up. Hands up," in his signature hypnotic, rumbling voice.[1] In the course of his song "Incredible," the lyrics touched on women, drugs, sex, money, expensive possessions, and love—some of Future's favorite topics. People in the crowd danced along.

Future's album *HNDRXX* debuted at the top of the charts when he released it in February 2017.

> "[Future] looks less like an actual rapper than a movie star cast as one. Even leaked mug shots from his pre-fame hustling days look like outtakes from magazine shoots."[2]
>
> —*Brian Hiatt*,
> Rolling Stone *magazine*

MC

The initials MC often appear with the names of rappers, including Future. MC (also spelled emcee) is short for "master of ceremonies." In the world of rap, it means a skilled performer who can get an audience hyped up and into the music. MC can also stand for "mic controller" or "move the crowd." Not all rappers are considered MCs. As rapper Stic.man of Dead Prez said, "A rapper is to an emcee what an average street fighter is to a trained martial artist. They are both fighters but the degree and depth of their skill is very different."[3]

UNPRECEDENTED

Future's performance thrilled the audience of *Ellen*, a talk show hosted by comedian Ellen DeGeneres. With Future's performance, he joined an elite group of other hip-hop artists who had appeared on the Emmy Award–winning show, including Kanye West, Drake, Nicki Minaj, DJ Khaled, André 3000, and Kendrick Lamar. But something about Future's appearance was different. Just moments before Future took the stage, DeGeneres made an exciting announcement while introducing the young rapper: "Our next guest is attempting to do what no one else in rap has ever done: have two different number one albums released in back-to-back weeks."[4]

Just after his performance on *Ellen*, Future lived up to that record-breaking pronouncement. He did "the impossible," what no other artist in any musical genre had ever done. He released two albums in two weeks, and both rocketed to Number 1 on the *Billboard* 200 chart. His album *Future*, released in late February 2017, made it to the top spot, selling 140,000 copies in its first week. His album *HNDRXX* followed one week later, selling 121,000 copies by the end of the first week in March. They gave the artist his

IN GOOD COMPANY

The last artist to top the charts in two consecutive weeks with two different albums was folk group Simon & Garfunkel in 1968 with *Bookends* and *The Graduate*. But those albums did not debut at Number 1. Only eight artists besides Future have occupied *Billboard's* top two spots at the same time. The last was Prince, when *Very Best of Prince* and *Purple Rain* were at numbers one and two after his death in April 2016.

"Future is our bard for these . . . times—a rapper whose psychedelic mumbles have become one of the most pervasive sounds in pop. . . . He's a visitor from tomorrow. . . ."[5]

—Chris Richards, the Washington Post

Future and Kendrick Lamar perform at the 2017 BET Awards.

fourth and fifth consecutive Number 1 albums, following *EVOL*, *What a Time to Be Alive*, and *DS2*. As another first, Future topped the charts in back-to-back weeks with two albums. With the release of *HNDRXX* at Number 1, *Future* slid just one spot to number two.

ROAD TO STARDOM

It was a heady time for a musician who had started out on the streets of a tough Atlanta, Georgia, neighborhood, where he experienced poverty and sold drugs for most of his teen years. But in the spring of 2017, 33-year-old Future was riding high. In addition to *Future* and *HNDRXX*, the rapper had released five mixtapes, two solo albums, and a collaborative album with the rapper Drake, all between 2014 and 2016. Most were hits. According to Brian Hiatt of *Rolling Stone*, it was "a creative run pretty much unmatched in quantity and quality by any contemporary in any genre."[6]

Future was now a force in the world of hip-hop and among the top rappers. His live performances sold out. Rap fans recognized him as easily as they did Drake or Kanye West. Up-and-coming rappers were copying his unique sound, trying to match his success. Future felt the change. In a 2017 interview with radio DJ Zane Lowe, he

MIXTAPES VS. ALBUMS

Future began his career making mixtapes rather than albums. Both can be polished, original music, featuring a single artist and big-name guest artists. One difference between the two is the goal. Albums are produced by record companies and are intended to make money, whereas mixtapes are often given away for free by the artist. The goal of many mixtapes is to gain new fans and create buzz for the musician and upcoming tours or albums. For some artists, mixtapes allow them to be freer and more spontaneous with content since they do not have to deal with restrictions from record labels.

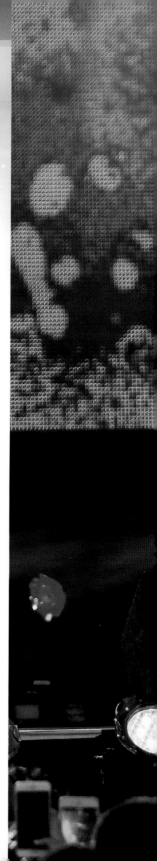

Future works the crowd at *Jimmy Kimmel Live* in April 2017.

said, "You definitely feel the shift in gears, like in the way people perceive you . . . new sponsorships, new partnerships, new tours, new offers."[7]

But along his journey were some big bumps. Future was still reeling from a failed relationship with R&B singer Ciara. A custody battle over their new son, other legal issues, and online feuds had pulled him away from his music. In addition, one triumph still evaded Future. He had yet to be nominated for a Grammy, arguably the most prestigious music award. Although his performance on *Ellen,* as well as other appearances on shows such as *Jimmy Kimmel Live* and *Saturday Night Live,* placed Future inside American living rooms, he was not well known by the general public. He knew he might never reach the kind of celebrity status enjoyed by some other rappers. But even Future was unsure whether that was what he truly wanted.

GROWING UP MEATHEAD

uture was born Nayvadius Wilburn on November 20, 1983, near Atlanta, Georgia. Wilburn was his mother Stephanie's last name. His father was not listed on the birth certificate. His dad did not play a big role in his life and left for good when Future was ten years old. Though Future's mom had a steady job as a 911 operator, there was never enough money. Future sings about eating cold SpaghettiOs from a can and heating their house with the stove.

Early on, friends nicknamed Future "Meathead" because they thought he had an oversized head. Later, he even recorded some music as Meathead before changing his nickname to Future. He grew up in Kirkwood, a neighborhood east of Atlanta. It was a rough neighborhood, hit hard by the crack epidemic of the 1980s.

Future with his mother, Stephanie Jester

ALL IN THE FAMILY

Because his mom worked, Future's great-aunt often babysat him at her home. It was a drug house, also known as a trap house. Future had a number of aunts and uncles who took drugs and sold them. His family had been street hustlers for two generations. While staying at his grandmother's at approximately the age of seven, robbers kicked in the door and tied everyone up. The criminal lifestyle did not mean much to Future at the time. "When you grow up in something," he told *Rolling Stone*, "you don't even know if it's bad or good. You just know that's how it is."[1]

While he was in third grade, Future heard a classmate rapping. The simple melody really clicked with Future, and he began to do his own rhyming. He also was affected by music with emotion, such as the hymn "Amazing Grace," which his grandmother sang around the house. He felt the pain and struggle in songs and would later insert them

NAYVADIUS

Future's influence extends beyond music. It may also be affecting first names. According to the U.S. Social Security Administration, only 14 babies born between 1880 and 2015 were named Nayvadius. But of those 14, seven were born in 2013.

into his own melodies. As a teen, he saw Jay-Z, Method Man, Redman, and DMX in concert in south Atlanta, and he decided rapping would be his chosen career.

Future decided to pursue rap after seeing artists such as Method Man, *left*, and Redman in concert.

ATLANTA, HIP-HOP HOTBED

"In Atlanta, there's no limitation to where you can take your music. You can be as creative as you want to be," Future told the *Washington Post* in 2016.[3] The emergence of Atlanta as the capital of hip-hop began with OutKast around 1995. It grew with the rise of rappers T.I., Gucci Mane, Jeezy, and Ludacris. Future and Young Thug have continued that dominance. One reason so many rappers come from Atlanta is that it is a historically black city with a number of black colleges, including Morehouse, Spelman, and Clark. Young people go to college and tend to stay in the city once they graduate. Many of them are fans of rap music and fill local clubs, giving new artists a chance to be heard and grow a fan base.

But Future's life would first take a different path. When he was 14 years old, he wound up on the streets selling drugs like most of the rest of his family. When he was 15 years old, Future was robbed and shot in the right hand when he reached for the robber's gun. He still has the scar. "I was a beast after that," he said in an interview. "I was like an animal, ain't had no love for nobody."[2] Future was an excellent athlete and had played basketball when he started high school, but the injury put an end to his basketball career.

Future's mom had little patience for her son's

"I had to give the streets up to really make my way into music."[4]

–Future

The capitol of hip-hop, Atlanta is home to artists such as OutKast, *pictured*, Ludacris, Gucci Mane, and Future.

decisions and hated that he was selling drugs. He did the opposite of whatever she asked, and they often fought. By the time he was 17 years old, Future was no longer living with his mother and was staying with relatives and sleeping on their floors. He let the streets raise him.

By now he was earning more money than his teachers. Listening to them no longer made sense to Future. He dropped out of Columbia High School during his senior year. He was arrested several times and faced charges of receiving stolen property, possessing drugs, and failing to appear in court. He had a son when he was 18, but he did not participate much in the boy's life.

LUCKY BREAK

Future had a rough start, but he could rhyme, and he was still convinced he could make it as a professional rapper. He had known for a while he had a second cousin, Rico Wade, who was a successful rap producer and headed the production company Organized Noize. Future's grandfather talked Wade into meeting with his cousin. "My granddaddy was like, 'My grandson is into the streets, he needs to

NEW UNDERSTANDINGS

As a teen, Future was angry with his mother because he thought she was not being supportive enough. He later realized she was just showing tough love. They became close again when he was older. He later changed his mind about school, too. "I'm smarter today than I was then," he said in 2016. "If I was [as] smart as I am now, I would have asked for *more* work. I would have been reading more books. Just as much as I work in the studio now, I would have been in school that much."[5]

get out. . . . See what you can do with him.'"[6] Wade invited Future to his studio for a session. Future did a recording but then went back to the streets.

Future and Wade met again at a family funeral. The two talked, and Wade told Future he had been playing Future's unfinished song to other members of his production team, called the Dungeon Family. The Dungeon Family really liked it. Wade invited Future to the Dungeon studio, near Atlanta, for another session.

THE DUNGEON

Rico Wade's Organized Noize, which began in the early 1990s, was more than a production company. One reporter noted, "They were artist developers, mentors, big brothers, and player-partners to everyone under the Dungeon Family umbrella."[7] The hip-hop family had a big influence on Future, who had DUNGEON and FAMILY tattooed on his forearms when he was still a teen. Early on, the original Dungeon studio was located in the unfinished, dirt-floor basement of Wade's mother's house in the Lakewood Heights neighborhood of Atlanta. It changed locations through the years and was located in Wade's mansion when Future did some of his recording.

Future took advantage of the opportunity. He sang a rap he called "Trapstar." Future began spending most of his time at the studio, and he moved in with Wade. It would be three or four months before Future returned to Kirkwood and life on the streets.

A Dungeon Family reunion—including Andre 3000, *left*, and Big Boi of Outkast—brings a packed house at the 2016 One Music Fest.

TRAP MUSIC

The title of Future's song "Trapstar" refers to a *trap*, street slang for a place where drugs are sold. Some rap, including Future's, is characterized as trap music. It's derived from the lifestyle of drugs, gangs, and "drank" (a mixture of soda and cough syrup). It got its start with hip-hop groups from the early 1990s, such as UGK and Three 6 Mafia, and continued with Atlanta-based Gucci Mane, Young Jeezy, and others. Los Angeles, California, has its own version of trap, with UZ and Baauer. The sound has been described as being one-third hip-hop, one-third dance music, and one-third dub, which is a remix of existing recordings.

Future was impressed by his cousin's mansion, which he saw as evidence that his life could change for the better. "You never think a person can live like this," Future said in a 2016 interview. "And he got this from creating music. Man, I just dropped out of . . . high school! And it put tremendous pressure on you, 'cause . . . this is what you have to work towards."[8] At last, Future had the right connections to break into the world of rap. He also had the desire. Time would tell if he had the talent.

LIFE IN THE DUNGEON

From the outset, Future knew he wanted to pursue a solo career. But Rico Wade believed it was important for Future to learn the business. Plus, Wade did not want to upset the older musicians in the Dungeon Family who were waiting patiently for their own shots at stardom. Wade teamed Future with four other musicians to create a group called Da Connect. They released *Dungeon Family 2nd Generation* in 2003. The album did not make much of a splash, and the group soon disbanded. But Future stayed at the studio, writing for other artists. One of his first assignments was creating a hook for "Blueberry Yum Yum," a track Ludacris would release on his 2004 album *The Red Light District*. The single became a big success.

By the time Future got behind a microphone as part of Da Connect, other members of the Dungeon Family— which included OutKast and Goodie Mob—were his

Future claims his real name, Nayvadius, means "king" in Greek. He set his sights on becoming a king of rap.

biggest supporters. "I was, like, 17. Everyone else was 25, 26, 32," Future told the *Washington Post*. "Everyone's saying, 'You're the future of the Dungeon, you're the future of the Dungeon. Future, future, future.'"[1] He used either his nickname Meathead or his real name Nayvadius on releases until 2004, when he began going by Future.

HOOKS

Use of the term *hook* began in the early days of songwriting and describes the part of a song that grabs—or hooks—the listener. It is a catchy blend of lyrics, rhythm, and melody. The hook most often comes in the chorus, the part of a song that's repeated after each verse. The best hooks seem familiar from the first time they are heard. Songwriters like hooks, because they serve as a way to keep music in people's minds and can increase a song's popularity.

LOW POINTS, HIGH POINTS

When paid opportunities dried up at the Dungeon, Future went back to Kirkwood and his old life of selling drugs. He spent time with his friend Rocko, another Kirkwood rapper. The two bounced ideas off of each other and lived fast and hard. Future continued to work in the studio when he could, eventually finding a new crew of Atlanta producers, including Mike WiLL Made-It, Zaytoven, DJ Spinz, Metro Boomin, and 808 Mafia.

One of Future's first successes was the hook he created for Ludacris's hit single "Blueberry Yum Yum."

Future's first release was the mixtape *1000*, which came out in the summer of 2010. It marked a turning point away from his life on the streets. "All my thoughts was

MAN OF MANY NAMES

There are various theories why Future chose the name Future. One is that Rocko, a fellow rapper and producer, urged Future to change his name when he signed onto Rocko's A1 Recordings label. Rico Wade thought it came from a song idea. Others, including Future, say it was from his friends in Wade's recording studio who kept calling him "the future of rap."[4] Future also goes by the nicknames Future Hendrix, Astronaut Kid, and Super Future.

"But that *Dirty Sprite* . . .
I was hearing it in other
[people's] cars and I'm like,
'That's my lil' cousin!' At that
point I knew it was on."[5]

—*Rico Wade, music producer*

illegal, that's what I did up until I dropped *1000*," he said in an interview. "I woke up [proud] today like, man, I ain't gotta do nothing illegal."[2] The single "Notice Me" gained airtime on Atlanta radio stations.

After *1000* came the mixtape *Kno Mercy*, also released in 2010. *FDU & Freebandz*, *True Story*, and *Dirty Sprite* followed in 2011. The mixtapes caught on with fans and built an underground following. Future performed at clubs, earning approximately $7,500 a show, and showing poise "remarkable for an artist with such limited exposure," noted Felipe Delerme of music magazine the *Fader*.[3] But it was singing as a guest on rapper Y.C.'s single "Racks," released in 2011, that earned Future the most national radio airplay of his early career. The recording landed in the Top 10 on the *Billboard* Hot 100 chart and proved to be another milestone. "I'm telling you, after I made 'Racks,' I knew how to make a hit," Future said. "It wasn't even my song but I knew what I was doing. I just felt it like something was different."[6]

"Tony Montana," from his *True Story* mixtape, was Future's first official single. He described it as "music with no limits. . . . I'm being real. You listen to the content and you know I'm being true to the streets."[7] The single became a hit, peaking at 22 on the *Billboard's* Hot 100 top singles list. Future was generating real buzz. He appeared on the cover of the *Fader* at the end of 2011 and was included in the annual freshmen issue of the hip-hop magazine *XXL* in

MUSICAL INFLUENCES

After singing the hook on Y.C.'s single "Racks" in 2011, Future realized just how much people respond to melodies. As a result, he began listening to and watching more pop singers in addition to other rappers. He noticed that artists such as Lady Gaga, Bono, Rick James, and Tina Turner could get 50,000 people in a stadium to sing along. Growing up, Future listened to a lot of musicians, including Barry White, Marvin Gaye, Soulja Slim, Ice Cube, and Limp Bizkit.

Mike WiLL Made-It is one of several music producers Future collaborates with.

> "Future's appeal owes much to his ability to incorporate melody into songs about the perils of chasing street money and getting high as a coping mechanism."[8]
>
> *—Felipe Delerme, the* Fader

early 2012. Record labels began bidding for his attention, wanting to cash in on this new talent.

By 2011, Future's friend Rocko was enjoying a successful hip-hop career and had started his own record label, A1.

Future signed with the label to release his first six albums. But Future would change his mind and sign a deal with another company. The incident would result in an ongoing lawsuit filed by Rocko and an end to their friendship.

A BIG SIGNING

Though life in the Dungeon had passed, it provided Future with another critical connection. L. A. Reid was the founder of LaFace Records and produced many of the big hits from the Dungeon Family, including OutKast's 1994 Grammy Award–winning album *Speakerboxxx/The Love Below*. In July 2011, Reid joined Epic Records as its new chairman and CEO. He knew Future from his

FEUD WITH ROCKO

Rocko filed a $10 million lawsuit against Future in 2016. The suit alleged that Future breached his contract with Rocko's A1 label in 2011 by signing with the record label Epic and sidestepping his deal with A1. Rocko was seeking a 25 percent commission on all advances Epic paid to Future, in addition to 20 percent of Future's earnings on touring, endorsements, and other income. The total amounted to $10 million.[9] Future filed a countersuit, alleging Rocko owed *him* money. The two rappers feuded online, exchanging angry remarks on Twitter and Instagram. Afraid that Future would quickly spend all of the earnings from his 2017 Nobody's Safe Tour, Rocko asked a judge in May 2017 to put $5 million of those earnings into escrow, so Future could pay off the lawsuit if it went in Rocko's favor. As of October 2017, the lawsuits had yet to be decided.

time with Rico Wade. Reid signed Future in September 2011 as his first rap artist.

BIG AND SMALL LABELS

Three major record labels make up 80 percent of the world's music market—Sony BMG, Universal Music Group, and Warner Music Group. Each of these companies has subsidiary companies, or smaller labels, that sign their own artists. For example, Epic is a subsidiary of Sony BMG. In some cases, the subsidiaries might offer distribution deals to even smaller labels. This is the case with Future, whose albums produced by his Freebandz label are distributed by Epic.

Then 25, Future felt like working with Reid was the perfect way to move his career forward. "If you sign to a major label," he told *Billboard*, "you don't want to be on a big roster and be forgotten about."[10] As part of the deal with Epic, Future was given a large cash advance, and the record company would distribute the albums produced by Future's own record label, Freebandz, which he founded in 2011. Soon Future would begin signing artists to produce. His star was definitely rising.

VERGING ON STARDOM

Future had a few hits under his belt by 2012. More fans and critics were paying attention to the rapper from Atlanta and understanding his music. When Future released his debut album, *Pluto*, on April 17, 2012, Chris Richards of the *Washington Post* described it as "a collection of street-corner narratives Auto-Tuned into warbly, melodic, big-tent singalongs."[1] Jody Rosen of *Rolling Stone* said that with *Pluto*, "Future did the improbable, combining Auto-Tune, Afro-futurism, power-ballad schlock, and a demented rap-singing style to make one of the most potent, and most enjoyably whacked-out, hip-hop albums in recent memory."[2]

The album sold fairly well, with more than 40,000 moving in the first week.[3] A number of tracks got good radio airplay, including "Magic," "Same Damn Time," and "Tony Montana." Fans agreed that *Pluto* was

Pluto was the start of a string of hits for Future.

"I put together a classic."[4]
−Future, referring to his album Pluto

Future covered themes ranging from love to outer space on *Pluto*.

something special. The album peaked at number two on the R&B/Hip-Hop Albums chart. His love ballad about finding the perfect woman, "Turn on the Lights," reached number two on the R&B/Hip-Hop Songs chart.

A few music superstars also took notice. Beyoncé said "Tony Montana" was one of her favorite songs. Rihanna liked the album so much that she asked Future to sing on the track "Loveeeee Song" for her album *Unapologetic*. That collaboration introduced the rapper to a new pop audience, which he welcomed. He was first and foremost a rapper, but he considered himself a trailblazer and did not like getting locked into any categories.

Impressed by the enthusiastic response, L. A. Reid of Epic Records paid Future to rerelease *Pluto* with three new tracks and two remixes. The release, titled *Pluto 3-D*, came out in November 2012. On November 27, 2012, Future performed his remix single "Neva End" with R&B artist Kelly Rowland on the *Jimmy Kimmel Live* television show.

TO THE STARS

With the release of *Pluto*, Future showed his obsession with outer space. He has described his music as astronaut music. One explanation for the fixation is that his songs are big, timeless, and futuristic. The theme of space appears on almost every track on *Pluto*.

By the beginning of 2013, Future was hot, and getting hotter. In June, the hip-hop magazine *Complex* listed Future as number 9 of the 20 best young rappers, writing, "everything that Future has touched has turned gold."[5]

FOLLOW-UP TAPE AND A GOOD MATCH

Future was spending long hours in the studio working on his next album. In the meantime, he released a new mixtape, *Future Presents F.B.G. (The Movie)*, in January 2013. F.B.G. stood for Free Bandz Gang, Future's new family of artists under his Freebandz record label. The tape featured Freebandz artists and other guests, including Drake, Wale, Lil Wayne, and Busta Rhymes. Jody Rosen of *Rolling Stone* said it was "compelling," but added that it felt like a "placeholder" before Future's next big release.[6]

Future got help producing the mixtape from his collaborator, Mike WiLL Made-It, a rising star in Atlanta rap production. Mike WiLL had worked with Future on a few earlier songs, including "Turn on the Lights" and "Neva End." The partnership worked well. "Me and Mike clicked from day one," Future said in an interview.[7] Their plan was to first have Future focus on street rap, then go wherever inspiration took him, such as romantic

A SMART RAPPER

Benny Pough, executive vice president of Urban Music at Epic Records, was impressed by more than just Future's musical ability. Future understood the hip-hop business, who his fans were, and how to appeal to them. For example, Future did not come out with his love song "Turn on the Lights" until he already had some hits under his belt. "It wasn't the first-day, come-in-big chart-top record or a one-hit wonder," Pough told *Complex*. "'Turn on the Lights' hitting No. 1 showed where he is going as a real, complete artist."[8]

songs such as "Turn on the Lights." It would prove to be a winning formula with his growing fan base.

FIRST-TOUR MISSTEP

In October 2013, Future was scheduled to take part in his first tour, Drake's upcoming Would You Like a Tour? It would be Future's first chance to perform with the rap superstar. But that same month, Future gave a poor review of Drake's latest album. A *Billboard* editor quoted Future as saying, "Drake made an album that is full of hits, but it doesn't grab you. They're not possessive; they don't make you feel the way I do."[9]

Future insisted his comments were misquoted and misunderstood, but Drake was livid. He dropped Future

Future performed in rapper Drake's Would You Like a Tour? in 2013.

from the tour. Drake later changed his mind but asked Future to take a pay cut. Future declined and sued Drake for lost wages—approximately $40,000 per show, or

> "Through and through, Future is a chorus monster. He's mastered a formula of embedding such simple choruses into his songs that they're empowering."[12]
>
> —*Felipe Delerme, the* Fader

NOT A GOOD MATCH?

Not everyone approved of Future's relationship with Ciara. Some of Future's friends thought she was too "pop" and middle-class. Brittni Mealy, the mother of Future's son Prince, accused Ciara of breaking up Mealy's relationship with Future. She tweeted that Ciara was a "#hasbeen." But Future had high hopes he and Ciara would stay together, saying in an interview, "No one can ever come between us."[13]

$1.5 million total. They reconciled a few days later, and Future joined the tour, which kicked off in Pittsburgh, Pennsylvania.[11] Future said he loved being a part of the tour and enjoyed giving his fans a club experience.

BIG-NAME ROMANCE

Many of Future's song lyrics are about women. In real life, he'd had a number of relationships, some brief and others more long term. By 2013, he'd had three children with three different women. Then a serious, high-profile relationship entered his life. R&B singer Ciara and Future were scheduled to record at the same studio in Atlanta. The two met outside and took photos together. Ciara called him

Many of Ciara's hits are crunk&B music, a blend of R&B and crunk music, which itself is a fusion of hip-hop and electronic dance music.

Nayvadius, his real name, and gave him tips on posing for photos. The two hit it off. It was not long before they were dating.

Rumors of their relationship hit the tabloids in January 2013, when the two were seen having dinner together in Beverly Hills, California. Future confirmed they were an item during an interview with radio station Hot 107.9. "She's a beautiful woman," he said, "amazing, incredible, everything that comes with those words, that's what she represents."[14] The budding romance would rock his world, both personally and professionally.

LIFE IN
LOS ANGELES

Putting aside his deep Atlanta roots, Future moved to Los Angeles to be with Ciara. He dyed his dreadlocks blond and got into the whole LA scene, attending movie openings, awards shows, and even fashion shows with his new flame. In March and April 2013, the couple seemed inseparable, sharing loving notes and photos on the social media site Instagram. Future appeared in Ciara's sexy music video "Body Party." Ciara gushed about her feelings for Future, saying she did not care who knew they were together. "The way that he makes me feel, why not? If you love somebody you should express it."[1]

By August 2013, Future admitted in a radio interview that he was so in love that he was ready to pop the question. He did just that in October; he and Ciara were engaged. In January 2014, Ciara announced on the television program *The View* that she was pregnant with

Future and Ciara attend the Milan Fashion Week in Milan, Italy, in January 2014.

Future's child. She also discussed their wedding, saying she was enjoying every minute of planning it. "I think I'll be part bridezilla, I'm not going to lie," she joked to *People* magazine.[2] She wanted everything to be perfect.

BABY AND A BREAKUP

Their baby boy, Future Zahir Wilburn, was born May 19, 2014. But it would turn out to be a bright spot in an unraveling relationship. Future and Ciara broke up in August 2014. Rumors swirled that Ciara initiated the breakup because Future was having an affair with his wardrobe consultant. Future denied the allegations, insisting he had called off the engagement long before there were any rumors of cheating. "We grew apart," he told *HuffPost Live*.[3] He added that he had grown tired of

CIARA

Ciara Princess Harris was born on October 25, 1985, in Austin, Texas. An only child, she traveled the United States and Germany with her military parents before settling in Atlanta as a teen. After watching the pop group Destiny's Child on television, she decided to pursue a career in music. Her big break came after meeting Jazze Pha, a prominent Atlanta music producer. Atlanta's LaFace Records signed her in 2003, and she released her debut album, *Goodies*, in 2004. It was a huge hit and gained four Grammy nominations. Before her relationship with Future, the singer dated rap star Lil Bow Wow for two years.

life in Hollywood and had decided to go his own way.

HONEST

The year 2014 was noteworthy for more than just a celebrity relationship. On April 22, Future released his sophomore album, *Honest*. Originally titled *Future Hendrix,* he recorded it in 2013 while living in Los Angeles. Future anticipated the album would be a big hit. It was, somewhat. It debuted at number two on *Billboard's* 200 chart, behind the megahit soundtrack for the movie *Frozen*, but it sold only 53,000 units in its first week. That compared unfavorably with Drake, Eminem, and Jay-Z, whose most recent albums had

FUTURE'S CHILDREN

In addition to Future Zahir, Future's son with Ciara, the rapper has three other children. His son Prince was born in 2013 to Brittni Mealy. India J, a longtime girlfriend of Future's, gave birth to their daughter, Londyn, in 2009. Jessica Smith, another of Future's former girlfriends, is the mother of a son born in 2002. According to Future, one reason he wants to be successful is so he can take care of his children. "I'm just looking for stability and longevity," he told *Rolling Stone*. "I'm really doing it for stability for my kids."[4]

"If [my music] happens to end up on the Top 40 or the pop charts, it doesn't mean I meant to go pop. It's just where the music took me."[5]

–Future

all topped more than 500,000 in their first weeks.[6]

Honest was notable for its guest artists and collaborators. "Real and True" featured Miley Cyrus and Mr. Hudson, a British pop singer; the two also made a video with Future. Besides Cyrus and Hudson, Nicki Minaj, Kanye West, and the DJs Metro Boomin, DJ Spinz, and TM88 were also featured. The album had some edgy street tracks, such as "Move That Dope," but other tracks had a pop vibe.

Critical opinions were mixed. Some liked the album's different sound. In describing *Honest*, Christopher Weingarten of *Rolling Stone* wrote that it "bristles with confessional lyrics, and a raw, hard-edged, unpolished energy that recalls a mixtape hustler, not an android crooner."[7] Others complained that after the noteworthy debut of Future's first album, *Pluto*, *Honest* was a disappointment. Jeff Weiss of *Complex* thought it was inconsistent and awkward. Jon Caramanica

Ciara and son, Future Zahir, visit Russell Wilson at the Seahawks' football training camp.

ON TOUR

Future went on tour in 2014 after the April release of his sophomore album, *Honest*. The tour kicked off on May 23 in Milwaukee, Wisconsin, and ended July 12 in Montreal, Quebec, Canada. In announcing the tour, Future said, "I'm excited to finally hit the road to share my new album *Honest* with the fans. It's been a long time coming."[9]

of the *New York Times* noted that, while Future is "generally magnetic" on the album, the second half lacked intensity.[8]

FEELING ADRIFT

Though his romance with Ciara had ended, they were not done with each other. In April 2015,

Ciara was seen dating NFL quarterback Russell Wilson. Photos released online of Wilson pushing Future's son in a stroller angered Future. It appeared to him that Wilson was playing "daddy," when Future thought he had no right to be. Future and Ciara exchanged angry barbs in interviews and online as the issue of custody of their son made its way through the courts. Ciara also filed a libel suit against Future for online statements he made about her.

While accused of wishing for her to fail, Future told *Rolling Stone* in 2016, "[Ciara] being successful, her being happy, helps." He said the photos with Wilson upset him because, "That's my son forever. My son is going to be able to read this. He's going to be able to look at those pictures."[10]

"REAL AND TRUE"

Future had positive things to say about working with Miley Cyrus on the single "Real and True," from his album *Honest*. He said she fell in love with the song when she first heard the hook. She sang her vocals, and then Future wrote verses to go with them. "Miley is really cool and down-to-earth," he told *Rolling Stone*. "She's always fun to be around and I'm always cracking up when I'm on set with her."[11] Future also revealed the song was about his relationship with Ciara and trying to capture his feelings for her.

The breakup and lukewarm response to *Honest* left Future feeling adrift. He worried the public and media reaction would leave him looking like a joke. DJ Esco, a friend and colleague from Atlanta, urged Future to return to his hip-hop roots, focus on verses rather than hooks, and turn his emotional pain into music. Future would do just that.

ALL IN HIS BRAIN

According to Future, he finished *Honest* two years before its 2014 release—in his head. He would come up with bits and pieces of music, such as a beat, a melody, or a hook. Then he would add whatever else was needed. "It's just about putting it together. Like a puzzle," he told *Billboard* magazine.[12]

BACK TO BASICS

Future moved back to Atlanta and worked long hours in the studio, returning to the hip-hop basics he, and his fans, seemed to prefer. Gone were the multiple big-name collaborators and various musical styles featured on *Honest*. This was Future, pared down to the streets again.

From October 2014 to March 2015, Future released a trio of mixtapes: *Monster, Beast Mode*, and *56 Nights*. It was quite a change from the two-year wait between 2012's *Pluto* and 2014's *Honest*. Future had a lot of music in his head, and he wanted to get it out. As he told National Public Radio (NPR) in 2014, "I'm not gonna just hold my music for another year. I can't. . . . I'm putting my music out every three months. I'm doing it. I'm dropping bombs."[1]

Future teamed with producer-DJs Metro Boomin and Zaytoven on these tapes. Although the releases did not get him into the Top 25, Future did propel himself beyond

Future has received several nominations for the BET Awards since he began performing.

Future teamed up with guest rapper Lil Wayne on his mixtape *Monster*.

HIP-HOP PRODUCERS

Perhaps more so than in other musical genres, hip-hop is a collaboration between the artist and producer. The producer sits in the control room of a recording studio and plays music with a unique beat or tone, and the rapper sings over it. Producers have their own sound, and the best can get prominent credit on albums.

"The most calmest place I can be is the studio. And like, I stay in there 'cause I know when I come out it's back to reality."[3]

—Future

the rest of the hip-hop pack with frequent good music. In the mixtape *Monster*, which he released in October 2014, he embraced what he thought other people hated about him. It had just one guest artist, Lil Wayne, and a much darker tone than *Honest*. The lyrics touched on drugs, casual sex, spending a lot of money, and nasty breakups.

The tape got good buzz with his core rap audience. *XXL* called it one of the best mixtapes of the year. *Slant* magazine gave it three and a half stars out of five, calling it "One of the most vivid, convincing, and plain, honest accounts of post-relational malaise to be expressed through pop in recent years."[2] Though sales were not brisk, the tape

confirmed for Future that his place was in Atlanta as a rapper, not in LA as a rap-pop crossover.

Future released *Beast Mode* three months later, in January 2015. It was short, at 27 minutes, and he recorded it in just two to three days. The same themes from *Monster* were again present, especially failed relationships. Then, in his mixtape *56 Nights,* Future went even darker. It released in March 2015 and featured DJ Esco. Lyrics referred to heavy drug use and reliance on drugs. It spawned the hit single "March Madness," which includes references to police shootings of African Americans. Critical response was mixed. *Rolling Stone* thought highly enough of the tape to name it the twelfth-best rap album of 2015. Sheldon Pearce of *Pitchfork* was not as enthusiastic and complained about Future's drug use, writing *"56 Nights* is an unfiltered look at life through the eyes of a wasted Future." *Spin* seemed to agree that Future sounded "haggard and warbled" on the tape. But, they added, "He's rhyming tighter than ever here, turning phrases with a flick of the wrist."[4]

REACHING THE TOP OF THE CHARTS

Future quickly followed those three mixtapes with his third studio album, *DS2* (short for *Dirty Sprite 2*), in July 2015. He was still searching for the record that would finally push him into hip-hop's upper ranks. On *DS2*, Future did not stray far from his street themes of drugs, women, and spending money. A year after splitting from Ciara, their legal battles continued, and angry break-up lyrics laced his songs. Future also included lyrics about wanting to separate himself from his pop exploration on *Honest*.

Kris Ex of *Billboard* gave the album three and a half stars out of five and noted the despair in the music. "There's no civility

56 NIGHTS

The title of Future's mixtape *56 Nights* refers to the number of days his DJ on the tape, Esco, spent in a Dubai jail in the United Arab Emirates. Esco was on a trip to the 2014 Abu Dhabi Grand Prix to perform in concert with Future. Esco was arrested at the airport for marijuana possession. While in jail, he learned about Islam and made friends with a warden who helped get him released. *56 Nights* was the first project DJ Esco worked on after his release.

Future with DJ Esco, his guest artist on the mixtape *56 Nights*

to be found here," he noted. "[It's] as if [Future's] selling a happiness he doesn't believe in."[5] Micah Singleton of the *Verge* said the album felt too calculated and fell short

of Future's three mixtapes, which he believed had more "quality and restraint."[6]

Other critics were more enthusiastic. *Rolling Stone* ranked *DS2* as the fifth best rap album of 2015, writing,

Future and Drake proved to be a good combination on tour.

BILLBOARD CHARTS

Each week, *Billboard Magazine* publishes a list called the *Billboard* 200. It ranks the most popular albums of the week in all musical genres, based on retail album sales and online streaming. *Billboard* also publishes the all-genre weekly Hot 100, which ranks individual songs based on a tabulation of sales, radio airplay, and online streaming. The Hot Rap Songs list is similar to the Hot 100, but it is limited to rap songs only.

"[Future] is as compelling as ever, if not more so."[7] It also inspired fans. *DS2* became Future's first Number 1 album on the *Billboard* 200 charts, selling 151,000 units in its first week.[8] That more than doubled his best week for any previous release. The single "Commas" peaked at Number 11 on *Billboard's* Hot Rap Songs chart. The rapper was building a name for himself.

2015 TOURS

In between working in the studio and releasing music, Future found time to perform in concerts. First, he joined rap star Drake on Drake's Jungle Tour. It opened in Houston, Texas, on May 24, 2015, and included just six dates.

In July, Future began offering free Salute the Fans concerts to promote his upcoming *DS2* album.

Cities on the tour were to include New York City, Atlanta, Los Angeles, and Chicago, Illinois. Concert details were released only the mornings of the shows. In Los Angeles, Future was scheduled to perform at the Roxy nightclub. But hundreds of fans flooded the venue, forcing the closure of Sunset Boulevard, where the nightclub was located. Sheriff's deputies in riot gear arrived to control the crowd, and the concert had to be canceled.

COLLABORATION WITH DRAKE CONTINUES

Future's packed year was not over yet. In September 2015, he partnered with Drake and released the album *What a Time to Be Alive*. It immediately shot to Number 1 on the *Billboard* 200 chart, selling 334,000 units in the first week.[9] It gave both Drake and Future their second Number 1 releases of the year. (Drake's first Number 1 album of 2015 was *If You're Reading This It's Too Late*.) They joined an elite group of artists to earn more than one Number 1 album within 12 months. The last to do so was the pop group One Direction in 2014. Ben Thompson of the *Guardian* newspaper gave the tape four stars out of five, calling it "uneven, but ultimately thrilling."[10] He said that Drake seemed energized by Future. Frazier Tharpe of *Complex* noted, "a week's worth of sessions yielded a nice bounty of music."[11]

By all accounts, 2015 was an amazing year for Future. He ended it with two Number 1 albums and a slew of new fans. As one reviewer noted, in 2015 Future was "your favorite rapper's favorite rapper."[12] He would try to keep the momentum going.

Future performs at a Salute the Fans concert in 2015 in Atlanta.

BIGGEST HITS

Future's 2015 was huge, both in terms of output and building his fame and fan base. But rather than take a break and give listeners time to digest his latest hits, the rapper started 2016 with another new release. In mid-January 2016, Future released the mixtape *Purple Reign*. For some reviewers, it felt like a spur-of-the-moment release. They thought it had a few nice tunes but felt it was really meant to hype his upcoming *Purple Reign* tour. The tour kicked off in Madison, Wisconsin, on February 17, 2016, and ended on March 19 in San Jose, California. Ty Dolla $ign was the opening act. The tour featured five big screens that showed images of some of Future's favorite lyric topics, including drugs, women, cops with guns, and money.

Future's next album, *EVOL* ("love" spelled backward), dropped three weeks after *Purple Reign,* on February 6.

Future performs at the 2016 BET Awards.

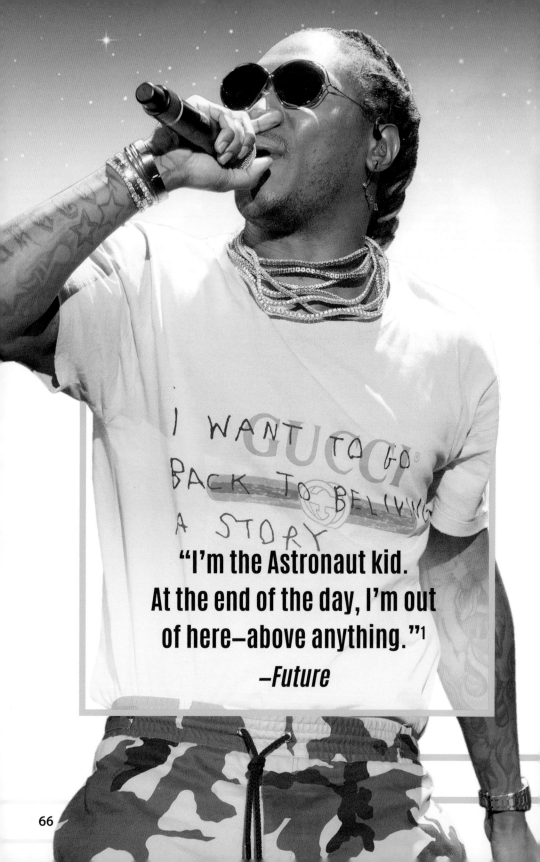

"I'm the Astronaut kid. At the end of the day, I'm out of here—above anything."[1]

–Future

It was a surprise release in a deal Future made with Apple to sell the album exclusively through Apple Music and iTunes. Craig Jenkins of *Billboard* magazine thought that the album was "allergic to romance," with even more of the unease Future had expressed on previous releases.[2] Musically, Jenkins praised the album's production by Metro Boomin, Southside, and DJ Spinz and admired how the album ventured into a new sound. It may not have been a big hit with every critic, but fans liked it. The album became Future's third Number 1 on the *Billboard* 200 chart.

With Future's three Number 1 albums coming within approximately six months of each other, it was the fastest accumulation of number ones for any artist

TOO MUCH OF A GOOD THING?

Zach Frydenlund, writing for *Complex*, noted that although Future's albums and mixtapes are always good, with so many releases within such a short period the rapper was overshadowing his own music and competing with himself. "Future doesn't have a quality control problem but more a quantity control one," Frydenlund wrote.[3] He urged Future to slow down and let fans enjoy what he had already produced.

The prolific Future was bursting with creativity.

2016 CONCERTS AND APPEARANCES

In the summer of 2016, Future and Drake toured together again, this time in The Summer Sixteen Tour. It launched July 20 in Austin, Texas, before traveling around the United States and Canada. It ended on September 17 in Vancouver, Ontario, Canada. Special guests included Roy Woods and DVSN. The tour made a total of $84 million and become the top-grossing hip-hop tour to date.[5] In addition to touring, Future made a number of television appearances in 2016. On March 5, he sang "March Madness" and "Low Life" (with The Weeknd) on NBC's *Saturday Night Live*. On April 15, he sang "Wicked" on Jimmy Fallon's *The Tonight Show*. He performed the same song for the BET awards show on June 25.

since 2010, when the cast of the television series *Glee* had three Number 1 soundtrack albums.

According to Jeff Weiss of *Complex*, *Purple Reign* and *EVOL* "lacked carbonation."[4] In the two releases, Weiss believed Future had failed to draw on the emotional vulnerability that made him unique. Critics and even other rappers wondered whether Future should slow down his output and conserve his creativity. As it would turn out, Future was about to take a yearlong break.

GROWING RECOGNITION (AND NOTABLE LACK THEREOF)

Beginning in 2011, Future was nominated for a number of awards by Black Entertainment Television's BET Awards, both in their general and hip-hop categories. In 2014, the single "Move That Dope" from his album *Honest* won BET's Hip Hop Award for Best Club Banger. The following year, his album *56 Nights* won for the best mixtape. In 2016, based on his string of 2015 hits, Future received nominations for several BET awards as well as awards from other organizations. He received nominations from *Billboard* Music Awards, iHeartRadio Music Awards, and American Music Awards, though he did not win.

> "I'm hitting [it] out the park—home run every time I step up."[6]
>
> –*Future*

There was one major exception to this recognition of Future's growing success—the Grammys. The Grammy Awards, considered by many to be the top music awards show of the year, overlooked Future for any category when 2016 nominations were announced in December 2015. In contrast, rapper Kendrick Lamar received 11 nominations,

and Drake had one. One reason for the snub, music insiders suggest, is that hip-hop artists such as Lamar and Drake focus less on drug use, sex, and profanity in their song lyrics, and more of their songs have a pop sound. Therefore, these artists have a broader appeal to the general public and to members of the Recording Academy, the organization that votes on the Grammys. Membership in the Recording Academy is made up of a broad range of music-industry professionals, representing many types of music.

JIMI HENDRIX

One of the nicknames Future calls himself is Future Hendrix. The nickname honors African-American guitarist and singer Jimi Hendrix, who broke color barriers in the early days of rock. Future also sees himself, like Hendrix, as a breakout artist. "The music I make," Future says, "I'm different."[7] Jimi Hendrix was born November 27, 1942, in Seattle, Washington. He learned to play the guitar as a teen and started his musical career as a backup guitarist for other musicians. His own band, the Jimi Hendrix Experience, debuted in 1966. His playing was explosive, exciting, and unmatched at the time. He died in 1970 at the age of 27 from a drug overdose.

"A MASTERPIECE"

Future began recording two new albums in the summer of 2016. He knew he wanted to release them both in 2017. He decided to stagger them a week apart so fans would have an opportunity to digest the first album, *Future,* before diving into his second, *HNDRXX. Future* was a look back at the artist's past, both musically and as a person. It is full of songs about the streets. *HNDRXX,* on the other hand, is a long distance from the streets and focuses on Future in the present. The album features two guest spots, The Weeknd and Rihanna, and the tone is mostly in minor key and introspective. "I'm opening you up to where I'm at," Future told *Billboard* magazine about *HNDRXX.* "It's about being vulnerable and not so cautious about what you say as far as your love life—if you was hurt or happy or in love."[8]

FUTURE ONLINE

Future posts as FUTURE/ FREEBANDZ @1future on Twitter and as of October 2017 had more than 4.5 million Twitter followers.[9] More than 11 million people were following him on Instagram, where he posts as Future Hendrix.[10] Future has occasionally carried out online feuds, including with rappers Young Thug and Rocko. Finding social media a big distraction, Future took a break from it in early 2017 so he could keep his mind on his music.

Future was released on February 17, 2017, and landed at Number 1 on the *Billboard* 200 chart. It was Future's fourth consecutive Number 1 album. Then, seven days later, on February 24, 2017, he released *HNDRXX,* which replaced *Future* in the Number 1 spot. Jeff Weiss of *Complex* said,

"*HNDRXX* is the highest incarnation of Future: that alchemy of joy, drugs, and pain that makes you unsure whether you want to cry or celebrate—probably both." Weiss added, "It may prove to be his masterpiece."[11] Mosi Reeves of *Rolling Stone* gave the album three and a half stars out of five, saying, "The warmth [Future] displays on *HNDRXX* is striking."[12] Future had again made magic in the studio.

Chapter EIGHT

UNIQUE STYLE

Future has said that he feels safest, and most at home, in the studio. It's also where he is most creative. If Future is angry or frustrated with life, the studio calms him down. It is a way for him to cope with fame, too. He feels a responsibility toward his fans and wants to make everyone happy, but that is difficult to do. The studio is a safe place to write, record, and hide. During his rare time off, he is thinking about what he's going to record next. Future says he got his strong work ethic from his earliest days with Rico Wade and the Dungeon Family. According to Wade, "Future's work ethic is ridiculous." But Wade admits he works the same way: "You live in the studio."[1]

In 2016, *Rolling Stone* magazine followed Future for an in-depth interview, part of which took place in a recording studio. With a beat playing in the background, Future paced, mumbled, and smoked for close to an hour.

Future with his second cousin Rico Wade, head of the Dungeon Family

Future's home is in the studio, where he can record several songs in one night.

Then he got in front of the microphone in the dimly lit vocal booth, swayed to the beat, and sang what came to him. His engineer that day, Seth Firkins, cued up the verse and looped the chorus, without direction from Future.

> "It's about that moment, you know what I'm saying? So every time I go in the studio, I'm trying to get that moment. . . . When I'm in the studio, I stay in the studio, like, sometimes 20 hours out [of] the day."[3]
> —Future

The rapper works quickly. He has been known to compose and record four songs from start to finish in one night. He works freestyle without writing anything down and just lets "the track talk."[2] Zaytoven, one of Future's producers, is amazed by his speed. "For somebody else to come in and see us doing the work, it would blow your mind," he told *Boombox* in 2015.[4] Zaytoven does not have to set aside weeks or months to work with Future like he does with other artists. He and Future record songs back to back and can get ten tracks done in one day.

Future's lyrics can come from anywhere, including something he saw on television or read. A conversation with a friend can spark a hook. He has said it is about being creative and putting an entire picture into words and music. But he has to do it in the spur of the moment, because the moment is gone so quickly. "So that's why you go in the booth and try to get those takes that you can't recreate," he told NPR. "If you try to do another take the same way, it wouldn't come out the same way."[5]

CRAZY IDEAS

Future finds inspiration for song lyrics from almost anywhere. Once, an idea came from his mother. She said something to Future as he left the house when he was in eighth grade. Years later, the words kept repeating in his head. When he got the opportunity, he went to the studio and put them on a track. "You get inspiration from the craziest places," he told NPR in 2014.[6]

Future enjoys being creative and finds inspiration everywhere.

THE FUTURE STYLE

Future's songs and style have been called melancholy.

Music critic Jon Caramanica in the *New York Times* noted

WORKING WITH OTHER ARTISTS

Although Future works with other artists, he has said that the legal issues it brings up are not always worth it. He said he prefers working with female artists because there is less ego involved. Mostly, he likes to work alone with the same producers from one recording to the next. He said that makes the process smoother, and that there are fewer problems that way.

"I'm the master of music, period. I feel like nobody in music can do what I do. The only people who can do what I do are from my camp and that's [André] 3000 and Cee-Lo [Green]."[7]

–*Future*

that Future tends to focus on a single idea, word, or phrase and then repeat it. Those words orbit around common topics, including women, relationships, life on the streets, drugs, and trappings of wealth, such as luxury cars, jewelry, and designer clothes. Caramanica observes that Future's vocal style can vary from sleazy to wistful to street tough, all in the same song.

On tracks Future records with DJ Metro Boomin, Chris Richards of the *Washington Post* said that "Metro likes to hang delicate chimes overhead, then bury land mines of bass down below, allowing Future's words to spread toward the horizon like melodious fog."[8] In a 2016 article for *Rolling Stone*, Brian Hiatt described Future's tone as a "digitally augmented baritone growl that sounds like he's gargling ones and zeros when the Auto-Tune is cranked up."[9]

AUTO-TUNE

Future is noted for his use of Auto-Tune. He began using the voice-altering device in his early recordings, liking the way it made his voice sound gritty and grimy. He was one of the first rap artists to use it. Others began copying him, such as Lil Durk and Meek Mill. Future did not mind the mimickers, calling them "his children."[10] Auto-Tune was what brought Future to the attention of many other rappers, including Quavo, of the group Migos. "I'd never heard nobody go so hard on Auto-Tune," Quavo told a reporter.[11] Future

SINGING RAPPERS

By definition, rap is rhyming speech chanted to background music—it is not sung. Rappers gradually began adding melodies into their raps because they wanted to push boundaries and appeal to a wider audience. Drake credits himself with being "the first person to successfully rap and sing."[12] His skill is even sometimes called "the Drake Effect."[13] Other rappers who sing melodies include Future, Lauryn Hill, André 3000, Ja Rule, 50 Cent, Nelly, and Kanye West.

Rappers including Meek Mill imitate Future's use of Auto-Tune.

has been criticized for overusing Auto-Tune. Some artists, such as Kanye West, use it occasionally to convey a certain emotion, but Future uses it all the time. In 2014, rapper T-Pain said in interviews that Future did not understand Auto-Tune or how to use it correctly.

In general, Auto-Tune has gotten a bad reputation from many musicians. Jay-Z's 2009 song "D.O.A. (Death of Autotune)" was highly critical of the device. Many music insiders worry musicians will never practice or try to improve their voices, since Auto-Tune can correct a singer's mistakes. But in the world of hip-hop, where artists use the device for weird vocal effects, proponents say Auto-Tune has brought a new level of excitement and has given rappers a way to be more melodic. Critics praised the haunting, melancholy sound Auto-Tune gave Kanye West's 2008 album, *808s & Heartbreak*. Critics have also praised Future's use of Auto-Tune. Lauren Nostro of *Complex* wrote, "It's a distinct style that other artists struggle to master, but Future finds it effortless."[14] It has become such a part of his musical style that Future may be using it for a long time to come.

HISTORY OF AUTO-TUNE

Like a spell-checker corrects spelling mistakes, Auto-Tune can fix a singer's slightly off-key notes. It is widely used for both live recordings and performances, eliminating the need for multiple takes to get a perfect sound. The digital device can also create special effects, making a voice sound robotic or warbling—the way Future uses it. The patent is owned by Antares Audio Technologies. Auto-Tune was invented by Andy Hildebrand, a geophysicist working for Exxon Oil Company. Hildebrand came up with the device to improve underground oil exploration by correlating sound waves. In the 1990s, Hildebrand began applying the tool to voices. The first popular use of its robotic sound-effect was on Cher's 1998 hit single "Believe." It has since become popular with many pop musicians and rappers.

FAMOUSLY UNKNOWN

F uture is popular with rap fans, and Future's musical style has heavily influenced other rappers, including Fetty Wap and Desiigner. On first listen, Future's producer, Mike WiLL, thought Desiigner's track "Panda" was by Future. Future has contributed to smash hits for Lil Wayne and Ace Hood. His style has been duplicated by younger rappers, such as Rich Homie Quan and Young Thug.

Future created his own unique hooks, sound, and flow, and since then, people have been trying to copy it. "The Future Hendrix sound . . . has become a part of Atlanta's DNA, as natural as breathing in the city's rap scene," wrote Elias Leight for *Billboard* magazine. "Youngsters like Young Thug and ILoveMakonnen have taken his blueprint . . . and run wild with it."[1] Having performed on songs for Miley Cyrus, Rihanna, and Justin Bieber, Future's influence also extends to pop. His "weird, emotive, gargle-groan," wrote

Future has a unique sense of style to match his unique music.

HOMES AND CARS

As of June 2017, Future owned a $2 million mansion in an upscale Atlanta suburb, a 50-minute drive from Kirkwood, where he grew up. He also owned a home in Miami, described by one observer as "a gleaming, ultramodern party pad with an almost surreally blue infinity pool that appears to flow into the ocean."[4] He also was planning to purchase a home in Los Angeles. In addition to nice homes, Future loves beautiful cars. He owns a $200,000 Range Rover SVR, a Bentley Bentayga SUV, and a Mercedes Maybach. But he would rather ride than drive. One of Future's uncles works as his chauffeur.

"The reason he has excelled in the music game is because he has a moral compass. He doesn't take advantage of people, and he can tell who's really down for him and who's not."[5]

—*Rico Wade*

one reviewer, "has become one of the most ubiquitous sounds in pop."[2]

2017 GRAMMYS

Despite all his influence and Number 1 albums, Future still lacked mainstream recognition in 2017. Perhaps nothing showed that more than his lack of Grammy nominations. After he was snubbed in 2016, the same thing happened the following year. Beyoncé received nine nominations in 2017, and Rihanna, Drake, and Kanye West earned eight each. Chance the Rapper got seven nominations, which the *LA Times* called "a remarkable number for any newcomer."[3] The *Times*

Through 2017, Beyoncé had been nominated for 62 Grammys and had won 22 of the awards.

went on to say that by nominating new and upcoming stars over music veterans, the Recording Academy was choosing innovation over tradition.

Some music insiders disagreed that the Grammys were spurning tradition. When Beyoncé's artistic achievement of *Lemonade* was passed over for Adele's popular *25*, people accused the Recording Academy of being culturally irrelevant.

GOLD AND PLATINUM

By selling more than 500,000 copies, Future earned gold certification from the Recording Industry Association of America (RIAA) for his albums *Pluto*, *Honest*, *EVOL*, and *Future*. *DS2* sold more than one million copies and was certified platinum.[6]

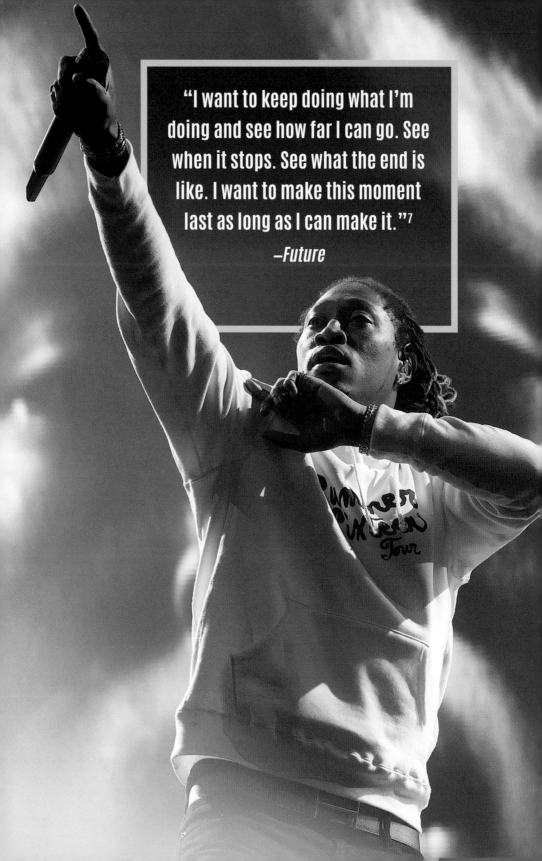

"I want to keep doing what I'm doing and see how far I can go. See when it stops. See what the end is like. I want to make this moment last as long as I can make it."[7]

–*Future*

Despite no Grammy nomination, Future is soaring high.

Billboard magazine noted Future's lack of nominations, as did Kanye West, who tweeted, "We the people need to see Future at the Grammys. . . . Not just me and [Jay-Z] in a suit."[8] Citing the Grammys' irrelevance and its lack of diversity, West, Drake, Frank Ocean, and Justin Bieber all skipped the February 12 awards ceremony.

For his part, Future has downplayed the Grammy snubs, saying the awards organization did not want to understand his music or what he was about. He was not going to let the controversy sidetrack him from his music. But the award does have a big influence on how far a musician can go and how much money he or she can potentially make. As Marcus Dowling of *HipHopDX* noted, "The music industry is an increasingly fickle business, and the mainstream credibility of having a Grammy-nominated song or album can go a long way to opening doors and ensuring Future's career sustainability."[9] L. A. Reid, chairman and CEO of Future's label, Epic Records, believes Future is sustaining his career just fine in his own way. By appealing to his core audience rather than pop-radio listeners, Reid thinks Future will come out ahead in the long run. "[M]y take is that it elongates his career," Reid told *Billboard*.[10]

MAKING MORE AND GIVING BACK

Future is an entrepreneur and does not shy away from the business side of the music industry. He loves clothes, and in 2016 he appeared on the cover of style magazine *GQ*, which named him one of the 12 "Most Stylish Men Alive." The magazine praised him for making hats popular again. Future sells a line of Freebandz clothing and accessories on his Freebandz website. In July 2016, Reebok announced Future would be the face of the campaign for their Instapump Fury OB

FREEBANDZ GANG

Future has connected a number of hip-hop artists and producers to his Freebandz record label since starting it in 2011. As of June 2017, people listed on the Freebandz website—in addition to Future himself—included Casino, DJ Esco, DJ X Rated, Doe Boy, Lil Don Loyal, Metro Boomin, Test, and Young Scooter. Future has stated that he prefers to make verbal agreements based on loyalty, rather than binding people with legal contracts.

athletic shoe. They held media events in London and New York, with Future as a special guest. The deal included a Reebok-Freebandz clothing line. And in September 2017, Future appeared in an ad campaign for clothing retailer the Gap with pop icon Cher.

Though some of Future's song lyrics may imply he is only interested in spending money on himself, the rapper also gives back. Future, along with his mother, Stephanie Jester, and his sister, Tia Wilburn, started the Free Wishes foundation "to deliver a message of hope, perseverance and resilience to our community by lending support and making dreams come alive."[11] The foundation held its first "A Winter Wishland" in 2012. The event gives clothing and toys to needy children in Atlanta. Through his

2017 CONCERTS AND APPEARANCES

In addition to Future's March 2017 performance on *Ellen*, Future appeared on *Jimmy Kimmel Live* in May 2017, where he sang "Mask Off" and "Used to This." After touring with Drake in 2016, and hot off his two Number 1 albums, Future decided to headline his own tour in 2017. The Nobody Safe Tour opened May 4 in Memphis, Tennessee. Opening acts included Migos and Young Thug. "This tour is about my whole journey," he told *Rolling Stone*, "so expect all the smashes."[12]

Future at the Winter Wishland community event in 2016

foundation, Future donated $25,000 to the Negro College Fund in 2016.[13]

THE FUTURE

Future has said in interviews that he is in a good place. "I'm happy with life now," he told *Billboard* in 2017. "I'm

happy with life, period."[14] He is also determined not to change himself to fit someone else's mold, the way he did during his relationship with Ciara. That includes his music and his lifestyle. In a 2014 documentary titled "I'm Just Being Honest," Future said his goal is to change people's lives with his music. With every song, he wants to inspire people to live the way they want to live.

Musically, Future denied in March 2017 that he had a follow-up to *HNDRXX* in mind. But that did not stop him from recording. On October 20, Future and Young Thug dropped a collaborative mixtape titled *Super Slimey*. Future also said he has thousands of songs in his head he has yet to release. His fans look forward to hearing them.

FEAR OF ROMANCE?

After his breakup with Ciara, romance became a complicated issue for Future. The thought of settling down again scared him and felt like a threat to his creativity. "I'm not broken," he said in an interview. "Why fix something if it's not broke? If I break it, and I try to fix it again, it might not be the same."[15] That doesn't mean he does not date. Future goes out with both celebrities and women he meets in his daily life.

1983

On November 20, Future (Nayvadius Wilburn) is born.

2003

Dungeon Family 2nd Generation, Future's first recording as a member of Da Connect, is released.

2004

Future's hook for Ludacris's single "Blueberry Yum Yum" is released and becomes a hit; Future starts going by the name Future instead of his nickname Meathead or real name Nayvadius.

2010

Future's debut mixtape *1000* is released.

2011

"Tony Montana," from Future's mixtape *True Story*, peaks at Number 22 on *Billboard*'s Hot 100 top singles list; in September, Future signs with Epic Records; Future starts his own record label, Freebandz.

2012

On April 17, Future's debut album, *Pluto*, is released.

2013

Future participates in his first tour, Would You Like a Tour?, with Drake; Future confirms he is dating R&B star Ciara. He moves to Los Angeles.

2014

On April 22, Future's second album, *Honest*, is released.

2014-2015

Beginning in October, and during the next six months, Future drops three mixtapes: *Monster, Beast Mode,* and *56 Nights*.

2015

Future's third album, *DS2*, comes out in July. It becomes his first Number 1 album.

2016

In January, Future's mixtape *Purple Reign* is released; on February 17, the *Purple Reign* tour kicks off in Madison, Wisconsin; on February 6, Future's fourth album, *EVOL*, is released. It shoots to Number 1; Future tours with Drake on the Summer Sixteen Tour.

2017

On February 17, Future's fifth album, *Future*, is released; on February 24, Future's sixth album, *HNDRXX*, drops one week after *Future*; on May 4, the Nobody Safe Tour opens in Memphis, Tennessee; on October 20, Future and Young Thug release *Super Slimey*, a collaborative mixtape.

BIRTH NAME
Nayvadius Wilburn

DATE OF BIRTH
November 20, 1983

PLACE OF BIRTH
Atlanta, Georgia

PARENTS
Stephanie Jester (mother)

EDUCATION
Attended Columbia High School; did not graduate

CHILDREN
- Future Zahir, a boy, born in 2014
- Prince, a boy, born in 2013
- Londyn, a girl, born in 2009
- A son, born in 2002, name not publicly known

CAREER HIGHLIGHTS
Future got his start with an Atlanta hip-hop production group known as the Dungeon Family, headed by his cousin Rico Wade. His fan base grew after the release of his first mixtape, *1000*, in 2010. Future followed that with a string of mixtapes and then his first album, *Pluto*, in 2012. It was a hit with fans and critics. By mid-2017, four of his albums had earned gold

certification, and *DS2* had earned platinum. His albums *Future* and *HNDRXX*, both released in 2017, reached Number 1 on the *Billboard* 200 list within two weeks of each other, a feat last accomplished in 1968 by Simon & Garfunkel.

CONTRIBUTION TO HIP-HOP

Future's unique style of singing-rap, melodic hooks, and Auto-Tune-altered voice has been widely copied. Rappers such as Young Thug, Ty Dolla $ign, and Desiigner have been influenced by Future's sound. Future has contributed to other artists' smash hits and has sung with pop artists such as Miley Cyrus, Rihanna, and Justin Bieber.

CONFLICTS

As a youth, Future sold drugs and lived a rough life on the streets, extending into the early years of his career as a rapper. His 2013–2014 relationship and later breakup with R&B star Ciara, and their custody battle over their son, caused a media stir. In addition to custody and libel lawsuits from Ciara, Future has been sued by rapper Rocko over a contract dispute. People have criticized Future for promoting drug use in his song lyrics and in his life. Despite his fame with his core rap audience, Future has yet to cross over into mainstream recognition.

QUOTE

"I want to keep doing what I'm doing and see how far I can go. See when it stops. See what the end is like. I want to make this moment last as long as I can make it."

—*Future*

GLOSSARY

ANDROID

A robot that looks human.

AUTO-TUNE MACHINE

A machine that digitally corrects sounds.

COLLABORATE

To work with someone else on a project.

CROONER

A male singer with a low voice.

CROSSOVER

Having success in a different musical style.

ELITE

A group that is better than the rest.

ENDORSEMENT

A public announcement of approval for someone
or something.

ESCROW

Funds held by a third party.

GENRE

A category of artistic composition, such as in music, characterized by similar styles, forms, or subject matter.

MALAISE

A feeling of depression or unease.

MILESTONE

An important point in time.

NARRATIVE

A story.

OPIOID

A drug that acts on the body like opium.

REMIX

A new and different version of a previous recording.

SUBSIDIARY

A company that is owned and largely controlled by another company.

SELECTED BIBLIOGRAPHY

Muhammad, Ali Shaheed, and Frannie Kelley. "Future: 'You Gotta Step Outside the Box to Reach the People.'" *NPR*. NPR Music, 29 Apr. 2014. Web. 9 Sept. 2017.

Ringen, Jonathan. "Atlanta Rap Hero Future on Making Chart History and Kicking It With 'Superstar Females.'" *Billboard*. Billboard, 23 Mar. 2017. Web. 9 Sept. 2017.

Weingarten, Christopher. "Future: How Hip-Hop's Paranoid Android Became a Robocroon Superstar." *Rolling Stone*. Rolling Stone, 14 Apr. 2014. Web. 9 Sept. 2017.

FURTHER READINGS

Burling, Alexis. *Drake: Hip-Hop Superstar*. Minneapolis: Abdo, 2018. Print.

Cummings, Judy Dodge. *The Men of Hip-Hop*. Minneapolis: Abdo, 2017. Print.

Hill, Laban Carrick. *When the Beat Was Born: DJ Kool Herc and the Creation of Hip Hop*. New York: Roaring Brook, 2013. Print.

ONLINE RESOURCES

Booklinks
NONFICTION NETWORK
FREE! ONLINE NONFICTION RESOURCES

To learn more about Future, visit **abdobooklinks.com**. These links are routinely monitored and updated to provide the most current information available.

MORE INFORMATION

For more information on this subject, contact or visit the following organizations:

ATLANTA CONVENTION AND VISITORS CENTER
233 Peachtree Street NE, Suite 1400
Atlanta, GA 30303
404-521-6600
atlanta.net

Check out the current hotbed of rap, where Future got his start.

THE BRONX TOURISM COUNCIL
851 Grand Concourse
Bronx, NY 10451
718-590-3518
ilovethebronx.com

Visit the home of hip-hop—the South Bronx, New York.

EPIC RECORDS
550 Madison Avenue, Floor 6
New York, NY 10022
212-833-8000
epicrecords.com

Epic is the record label of Future and a number of other hip-hop artists.

SOURCE NOTES

CHAPTER 1. "INCREDIBLE"

1. Jon Blistein. "Watch Future's Energetic 'Incredible' Performance on 'Ellen.'" *Rolling Stone*. Rolling Stone, 2 Mar. 2017. Web. 9 Sept. 2017.

2. Brian Hiatt. "Future: Syrup, Strippers and Heavy Angst with the Superstar MC." *Rolling Stone*. Rolling Stone, 29 June 2016. Web. 9 Sept. 2017.

3. "MC vs. Rapper: What Is the Difference?" *Sunday World*. tiso blackstar, 21 Nov. 2014. Web. 9 Sept. 2017.

4. Jon Blistein. "Watch Future's Energetic 'Incredible' Performance on 'Ellen.'" *Rolling Stone*. Rolling Stone, 2 Mar. 2017. Web. 9 Sept. 2017.

5. Chris Richards. "How Future Makes Us Feel the Slow, Cosmic Push of Time." *Washington Post*. Washington Post, 9 Mar. 2016. Web. 9 Sept. 2017.

6. Brian Hiatt. "Future: Syrup, Strippers and Heavy Angst with the Superstar MC." *Rolling Stone*. Rolling Stone, 29 June 2016. Web. 9 Sept. 2017

7. "Future's Full Interview with Zane Lowe." *YouTube*. YouTube, 16 Feb. 2017. Web. 9 Sept. 2017.

CHAPTER 2. GROWING UP MEATHEAD

1. Christopher Weingarten. "Future: How Hip-Hop's Paranoid Android Became a Robocroon Superstar." *Rolling Stone*. Rolling Stone, 14 Apr. 2014. Web. 4 May 2017.

2. Nadine Graham. "Future Talks 'Pluto 3D,' Rihanna Collabo & Sophomore Album." *Billboard*. Billboard, 26 Nov. 2012. Web. 9 Sept. 2017.

3. Chris Richards. "Atlanta Rapper Gets Inspiration from Pop Singers as Well as Hip-Hop Artists." *Washington Post*. Washington Post, 13 Apr. 2012. Web. 9 Sept. 2017.

4. "Future." *SXSW*. SXSW, n.d. Web. 9 Sept. 2017

5. Brian Hiatt. "Future: Syrup, Strippers and Heavy Angst with the Superstar MC." *Rolling Stone*. Rolling Stone, 29 June 2016. Web. 9 Sept. 2017.

6. Felipe Delerme. "Future: Dungeons and Dragons." *Fader*. Fader, 13 Dec. 2011. Web. 9 Sept. 2017.

7. Rodney Carmichael. "Family Reunion." *Oxford American*. Oxford American, 29 Dec. 2015, Web. 30 Sept. 2017.

8. Brian Hiatt. "Future: Syrup, Strippers and Heavy Angst with the Superstar MC." *Rolling Stone*. Rolling Stone, 29 June 2016. Web. 9 Sept. 2017.

CHAPTER 3. LIFE IN THE DUNGEON

1. Chris Richards. "Atlanta Rapper Gets Inspiration from Pop Singers as Well as Hip-Hop Artists." *Washington Post*. Washington Post, 13 Apr. 2012. Web. 9 Sept. 2017.

2. Felipe Delerme. "Future: Dungeons and Dragons." *Fader*. Fader, 13 Dec. 2011. Web. 9 Sept. 2017.

3. Ibid.

4. Dan Rys. "Future Sued for $10 Million over Alleged Breach of Contract." *Billboard*. Billboard, 9 June 2016. Web. 9 Sept. 2017.

5. Felipe Delerme. "Future: Dungeons and Dragons." *Fader*. Fader, 13 Dec. 2011. Web. 9 Sept. 2017.

6. Chris Richards. "How Future Makes Us Feel the Slow, Cosmic Push of Time." *Washington Post*. Washington Post, 9 Mar. 2016. Web. 9 Sept. 2017.

7. Felipe Delerme. "Future: Dungeons and Dragons." *Fader*. Fader, 13 Dec. 2011. Web. 9 Sept. 2017.

8. Ibid.

9. Lauren Savage. "Future Talks 'Pluto,' Epic Record Deal & More." *Billboard*. Billboard, 16 Apr. 2012. Web. 9 Sept. 2017.

10. Nadine Graham. "Future Talks 'Pluto 3D,' Rihanna Collabo & Sophomore Album." *Billboard*. Billboard, 26 Nov. 2012. Web. 9 Sept. 2017.

CHAPTER 4. VERGING ON STARDOM

1. Chris Richards. "Atlanta Rapper Gets Inspiration from Pop Singers as Well as Hip-Hop Artists." *Washington Post*. Washington Post, 13 Apr. 2012. Web. 9 Sept. 2017.

2. Jody Rosen. "Future Presents F.B.G. (The Movie)." *Rolling Stone.* Rolling Stone, 30 Jan. 2013. Web. 9 Sept. 2017.

3. Keith Caulfield. "Future Earns His First No. 1 Album on *Billboard* 200 Chart." *Billboard.* Billboard, 26 July 2015. Web. 9 Sept. 2017.

4. Kory Grow. "Drake Fires Future from Upcoming Tour: Report." *Rolling Stone.* Rolling Stone, 15 Oct. 2013. Web. 9 Sept. 2017.

5. Insanul Ahmed, et al. "The 20 Best Rappers in Their 20s (Right Now)." *Complex.* Complex, 4 June 2013. Web. 9 Sept. 2017

6. Jody Rosen. "Future Presents F.B.G. (The Movie)." *Rolling Stone.* Rolling Stone, 30 Jan. 2013. Web. 9 Sept. 2017.

7. Max Mertens. "Future Inspired by Jimi Hendrix for Next Record." *Rolling Stone.* Rolling Stone, 28 Jan. 2013. Web. 9 Sept. 2017.

8. Lauren Nostro. "Future: To Infinity and Beyond." *Complex.* Complex, 3 Jan. 2013. Web. 10 Sept. 2017.

9. Nadine Graham. "Future Talks 'Pluto 3D,' Rihanna Collabo & Sophomore Album." *Billboard.* Billboard, 26 Nov. 2012. Web. 9 Sept. 2017.

10. Caitlin White. "OG Maco: 'Future Has Destroyed Countless Lives by Making It Cool to Be a Drug Addict." *Stereogum.* Billboard-Hollywood Reporter, 10 July 2015. Web. 9 Sept. 2017

11. Kory Grow. "Drake Fires Future from Upcoming Tour: Report." *Rolling Stone.* Rolling Stone, 15 Oct. 2013. Web. 9 Sept. 2017.

12. Felipe Delerme. "Future: Dungeons and Dragons." *Fader.* Fader, 13 Dec. 2011. Web. 9 Sept. 2017.

13. "Future and Ciara Get Engaged: See the Couple's Dating Timeline." *MTV.* Viacom International, 28 Oct. 2013. Web. 9 Sept. 2017.

14. Henna Kathiya. "Future Confirms that He's Dating Ciara." *MTV.* Viacom International, 24 Jan. 2013. Web. 10 Sept. 2017.

CHAPTER 5. LIFE IN LOS ANGELES

1. "Future and Ciara Get Engaged: See the Couple's Dating Timeline." *MTV.* Viacom International, 28 Oct. 2013. Web. 9 Sept. 2017.

2. Michele Corriston. "Ciara and Future End Their Engagement." *People.* Time, 14 Jan. 2017. Web. 10 Sept. 2017.

3. Allison Corneau. "Future on Ciara Split: 'I Felt Embarrassed for Her,' Insists Cheating Had Nothing to Do with Breakup." *US Weekly.* American, 14 July 2015. Web. 10 Sept. 2017.

4. Adam Fleischer. "Future Announces Tour: Is He Coming to You?" *MTV.* Viacom International, 2 Apr. 2014. Web. 10 Sept. 2017.

5. Jon Caramanica. "Future, the Voice of Hip-Hop Today." *New York Times.* New York Times, 23 Apr. 2014. Web. 10 Sept. 2017.

6. Brian Hiatt. "Future: Syrup, Strippers and Heavy Angst with the Superstar MC." *Rolling Stone.* Rolling Stone, 29 June 2016. Web. 9 Sept. 2017.

7. Chris Richards. "Atlanta Rapper Gets Inspiration from Pop Singers as Well as Hip-Hop Artists." *Washington Post.* Washington Post, 13 Apr. 2012. Web. 9 Sept. 2017.

8. Nathan S. "Did Future's 'Honest' Album Flop, and Why?" *DJ Booth.* DJ Booth, 1 May 2014. Web. 10 Sept. 2017.

9. Nadine Graham. "25 Facts You Probably Didn't Know about Future." *Boombox.* XXL Network, n.d. Web. 10 Sept. 2017.

10. Christopher Weingarten. "Future: How Hip-Hop's Paranoid Android Became a Robocroon Superstar." *Rolling Stone.* Rolling Stone, 14 Apr. 2014. Web. 4 May 2017.

11. Phillip Mlynar. "Future Shares 'Honest' Details, Is Happy on Drake Tour." *Rolling Stone.* Rolling Stone, 5 Nov. 2013. Web. 10 Sept. 2017.

12. Brian Hiatt. "Future: Syrup, Strippers and Heavy Angst with the Superstar MC." *Rolling Stone.* Rolling Stone, 29 June 2016. Web. 9 Sept. 2017.

CHAPTER 6. BACK TO BASICS

1. Ali Shaheed Muhammad, et al. "Future: 'You Gotta Step Outside that Box to Reach the People.'" *NPR.* NPR, 29 Apr. 2014. Web. 10 Sept. 2017.

2. Christopher Weingarten. "Future: How Hip-Hop's Paranoid Android Became a Robocroon Superstar." *Rolling Stone*. Rolling Stone, 14 Apr. 2014. Web. 4 May 2017.

3. Micah Singleton. "Review: Future's DS2 Isn't the Trap Opus We've Been Waiting For." *Verge*. Vox, 20 July 2015. Web. 10 Sept. 2017.

4. Sam C. Mac. "Future: Monster." *Slant*. Slant, 3 Nov. 2014. Web. 10 Sept. 2017.

5. Drew Millard. "SPIN Rap Report: Future Raps Way Past Pluto and Father Revives Snap." *Spin*. Spin, 29 May 2015. Web. 10 Sept. 2017.

6. Kris Ex. "Future Pledges Allegiance to Highs & Lows of Self-Medication on 'Dirty Sprite 2': Album Review." *Billboard*. Billboard, 21 July 2015. Web. 10 Sept. 2017.

7. Micah Singleton. "Review: Future's DS2 Isn't the Trap Opus We've Been Waiting For." *Verge*. Vox, 20 July 2015. Web. 10 Sept. 2017.

8. Christopher R. Weingarten, et al. "40 Best Rap Albums of 2015." *Rolling Stone*. Rolling Stone, 23 Dec. 2015. Web. 10 Sept. 2017.

9. Keith Caulfield. "Future Earns His First No. 1 Album on Billboard 200 Chart." *Billboard*. Billboard, 26 July 2015. Web. 9 Sept. 2017.

10. Keith Caulfield. "Drake and Future's Surprise Album Debuts at No. 1 on Billboard 200 Chart." *Billboard*. Billboard, 27 Sept. 2015. Web. 10 Sept. 2017.

11. Ben Thompson. "Drake and Future: What a Time to Be Alive Review—A Dynamic Pairing." *Guardian*. Guardian, 11 Oct. 2015. Web. 25 May 2017.

12. Frazier Tharpe. "Review: Future Lets Drake Hitch a Ride to Pluto for 'What a Time to Be Alive.'" *Complex*. Complex, 22 Sept. 2015. Web. 10 Sept. 2017.

CHAPTER 7. BIGGEST HITS

1. "Future Continues to Deny Drug Addiction." *DJ Booth*. DJ Booth, 29 June 2016. Web. 10 Sept. 2017.

2. Craig Jenkins. "Future Hits His Songwriting Stride on Surprise Album 'EVOL': Review." *Billboard*. Billboard, 8 Feb. 2016. Web. 10 Sept. 2017.

3. Jonathan Ringen. "Atlanta Rap Hero Future on Making Chart History and Kicking It with 'Superstar Females.'" *Billboard*. Billboard, 23 Mar. 2017. Web. 10 Sept. 2017.

4. Ibid.

5. Ibid.

6. Ibid.

7. Mosi Reeves. "Review: Future Lets His Sensitive Side Show on 'Hndrxx.'" *Rolling Stone*. Rolling Stone, 28 Feb. 2017. Web. 10 Sept. 2017.

8. Nathan S. "Hypocritical Young Thug Slams Future for Releasing Too Much 'BS Music.'" *DJ Booth*. DJ Booth, 3 Feb. 2016. Web. 10 Sept. 2017.

9. "FUTURE/FREEBANDZ." *Twitter*. Twitter, n.d. Web. 3 Oct. 2017.

10. "Future Hendrix." *Instagram*. Instagram, n.d. Web. 3 Oct. 2017.

11. Zach Frydenlund. "Future's 'Evol' Is Great, But Here's Why He Should Slow Down on Dropping New Music." *Complex*. Complex, 7 Feb. 2016. Web. 10 Sept. 2017.

12. "Summer 2017's Hottest Tours: Kendrick Lamar, Lady Gaga, Metallica and More." *Rolling Stone*. Rolling Stone, 25 May 2017. Web. 10 Sept. 2017.

CHAPTER 8. UNIQUE STYLE

1. Lauren Nostro. "Future: To Infinity and Beyond." *Complex*. Complex, 3 Jan. 2013. Web. 10 Sept. 2017.

2. Christopher Weingarten. "Future: How Hip-Hop's Paranoid Android Became a Robocroon Superstar." *Rolling Stone*. Rolling Stone, 14 Apr. 2014. Web. 4 May 2017.

3. Lauren Nostro. "Future: To Infinity and Beyond." *Complex*. Complex, 3 Jan. 2013. Web. 10 Sept. 2017.

4. Christopher Weingarten. "Future: How Hip-Hop's Paranoid Android Became a Robocroon Superstar." *Rolling Stone*. Rolling Stone, 14 Apr. 2014. Web. 4 May 2017.

5. Nadine Graham. "Zaytoven Speaks on Future's Work Ethic, Nicki Minaj's Early Days & Usher's Ode to Migos." *Boombox*. XXL, 23 Jan. 2015. Web. 10 Sept. 2017.

6. Lauren Nostro. "Future: To Infinity and Beyond." *Complex*. Complex, 3 Jan. 2013. Web. 10 Sept. 2017.

7. Jonathan Ringen. "Atlanta Rap Hero Future on Making Chart History and Kicking It with 'Superstar Females.'" *Billboard*. Billboard, 23 Mar. 2017. Web. 10 Sept. 2017.

8. Ali Shaheed Muhammad, et al. "Future: 'You Gotta Step Outside that Box to Reach the People.'" *NPR*. NPR, 29 Apr. 2014. Web. 10 Sept. 2017.

9. Ibid.

10. Nadine Graham. "Future Talks 'Pluto 3D', Rihanna Collabo & Sophomore Album." *Billboard*. Billboard, 26 Nov. 2012. Web. 9 Sept. 2017.

11. Chris Richards. "How Future Makes Us Feel the Slow, Cosmic Push of Time." *Washington Post*. Washington Post, 9 Mar. 2016. Web. 9 Sept. 2017.

12. Stephen Horowitz. "Drake Says He's the First Person to Successfully Rap and Sing." *HipHopDX*. HipHopDX, 27 July 2012. Web. 3 Oct. 2017.

13. Allison McCann. "The Drake Effect Is Real, But the Nicki Effect Is Bigger." *FiveThirtyEight*. FiveThirtyEight, 21 Dec. 2015. Web. 3 Oct. 2017.

14. Brian Hiatt. "Future: Syrup, Strippers and Heavy Angst with the Superstar MC." *Rolling Stone*. Rolling Stone, 29 June 2016. Web. 9 Sept. 2017.

CHAPTER 9. FAMOUSLY UNKNOWN

1. Elias Leight. "Future Doesn't Shy Away from Rumors on 'Monster' Mixtape: Listen." *Billboard*. Billboard, 29 Oct. 2014. Web. 10 Sept. 2017.

2. Christopher Weingarten. "Future: How Hip-Hop's Paranoid Android Became a Robocroon Superstar." *Rolling Stone*. Rolling Stone, 14 Apr. 2014. Web. 4 May 2017.

3. Randy Lewis. "With Nominees Like Chance the Rapper, the Grammys Look to the Future of Music." *Los Angeles Times*. Los Angeles Times, 6 Dec. 2016. Web. 10 Sept. 2017.

4. Ted Simmons. "Future, Jeezy and More Donate $25,000 Each to United Negro College Fund." *XXL*. XXL, 19 Dec. 2016. Web. 10 Sept. 2017.

5. Ibid.

6. Ibid.

7. "About." *FreeWishes Foundation*. FreeWishes Foundation, n.d. Web. 10 Sept. 2017.

8. Jonathan Ringen. "Atlanta Rap Hero Future on Making Chart History and Kicking It with 'Superstar Females.'" *Billboard*. Billboard, 23 Mar. 2017. Web. 10 Sept. 2017.

9. Ibid.

10. "Future's Self-Titled Album Goes Gold." *Rap-Up*. Rap-Up, 5 May 2017. Web. 10 Sept. 2017.

11. Brian Hiatt. "Future: Syrup, Strippers and Heavy Angst with the Superstar MC." *Rolling Stone*. Rolling Stone, 29 June 2016. Web. 9 Sept. 2017.

12. Ibid.

13. Natalie Weiner. "After Beyonce's Loss, Grammys Respond to Critics: 'Join the Academy and Be the Change You Want to See.'" *Billboard*. Billboard, 15 Feb. 2017. Web. 10 Sept. 2017.

14. Marcus Dowling. "Future Deserved a Grammy Nomination." *HipHopDX*. HipHipDX, 8 Dec. 2015. Web. 10 Sept. 2017.

15. Jonathan Ringen. "Atlanta Rap Hero Future on Making Chart History and Kicking It with 'Superstar Females.'" *Billboard*. Billboard, 23 Mar. 2017. Web. 10 Sept. 2017.

INDEX

Melissa Higgins is an award-winning author of fiction and nonfiction books for children and young adults. She has written more than 70 nonfiction titles that range in subject matter from character development and psychology to history, biographies, and science. Before becoming a full-time writer, Melissa worked as a school counselor and had a private counseling practice. When not writing, she enjoys hiking and taking photographs in the Arizona desert where she lives with her husband.